GW00731827

QUEF

Echo Of The Eternal Word

Fr. Tomislav Pervan, O.F.M.

FRANCISCAN UNIVERSITY PRESS
AND
SVETA BAŠTINA – DUVNO
1987.

Front Cover: From an original painting by Andelko Mikulic

The artist's depiction of Mary, Queen of Peace, is based upon his impressions and his experience of Mary while he was present with the visionaries during the time of apparition.

Mr. Mikulic depicts Mary as hovering over the ground, rather than standing on it. Her figure is beautiful; her beauty divine, not human.

The cross at the upper right locates the apparitions in the village of Medugorje. The colors and the design around Mary simbolize the situation of the world into which she has come; a world that is torn by sin world that is not beautiful. Mary penetrates this world and creates a space for herself, with her beauty and message of peace.

The basis of this work was an article published in ERNEUERUNG IN KIRCHEUND GESELLSCHAFT. Heft 25 IV/1985. It has been updated and revised by the author for publication in English by Franciscan University Press.

Published in the United States by
Franciscan University Press
Franciscan University of Steubenville
Steubenville, OH 43952
Published in Yugoslavia by
,,Sveta Baština'' — Duvno
Printed in Yugoslavia by TRO ,,Franjo Kluz'' — Omiš

INTRODUCTION

Father Tomislav Pervan is an extraordinary man in an extraordinary place at this time. The events taking place in St. James Parish, Medugorje, Yugoslavia are being watched throughout the world. Father Tomislav is responsible for overseeing and directing the life of this parish.

He, therefore, has an unique position from which to analyze what is transpiring. He can tell us how it looks from within and, as a holder of a doctorate in New Testament studies, he can interpret theologically what is happening in Medugorje.

As a man, Father Tomislav is energetic, humorous, joyful and practical. His ability to stop everything and greet me warmly and care for my needs whenever I would "drop in" is a reflection of his ability to maintain Franciscan simplicity and joy in a whirlwind of supernatural and natural activity in Medugorje.

Father Michael Scanlan, T.O.R.
President
Franciscan University of Steubenville

"I looked toward the hill, and saw a bright figine. I said, "Mirjana, look, the Madonna!" (From Ivanka's account of the first apparition.)

The Madonna appeared near the place of the central white cross on the hill, Podbrdo, behind and above the village of Bijakovici.

QUEEN OF PEACE
ECHO OF THE ETERNAL WORD

Anyone who has been confronted with a phenomenon for more than five years and has been able to observe it first hand is obliged and challenged to interpret it and then to explain the interpretation. This holds true of the phenomenon of the reported apparitions of the Mother of God in Medugorje to six visionaries, even though the reported apparitions have not yet received explicit ecclesiastical approbation. The Church proceeds cautiously in such matters, keeping her approbation and judgement in abeyance.

Nevertheless, the news of the apparitions and the messages of the Holy Virgin in Medugorje, Yugoslavia, have been circulating throughout the world since June 24, 1981, generating a growing response from day to day and bearing good fruit among thousands of pilgrims.

The message of Medugorje is being spread mainly by word

of mouth. Printed material serves only as a supplementary aid.[1] The testimony of eyewitnesses is overwhelming as a rule. I consider this manner of communication fundamentally Christian, Jesus-like, because the message about Jesus and His Word was initially articulated and transmitted orally, before it was written down.

Technology, too, has made its contribution to Medugorje. Even though the camera may misrepresent and distort a subject, it has rendered a service to the apparitions in Medugorje. The camera has captured the phenomenon, the moment and the duration of the ecstasy and recorded them for posterity. Such a presentation relies upon the moving, visual image and can tend toward the spectacular. However, it can be done accurately with perseverance. When we consider the matter closely, putting aside all ideological presuppositions, we can come to one conclusion only. Medugorje represents something quite extraordinary and paranormal. The events and the message captivate all who believe and who are open to the work of the Holy Spirit. Pilgrims are transformed in the process into people who live their faith courageously and conscientiously and who bear witness to it in a vital way.

The impressive scenes of the ecstasy, the apparitions, speak for themselves and have an overwhelming effect on those present, though they can perceive merely the externals of the event. The inner state, the captivation of the visionaries, remains hidden from view. The apparitions are experiences that are transcendental, inaccessible, holy, charismatic events that are hidden from us. The whole reality is at once so near and yet so far beyond our comprehension.

Ivanka
Ivankovic

Mirjana
Dragicevic

Ivan
Dragicevic

Vicka
Ivankovic

Marija
Pavlovic

Jakov
Colo

"We have seen the Madonna."

APPARITIONS OF THE MOTHER OF GOD IN MEDUGORJE

The events in Medugorje began with apparitions of the Mother of God on June 24th, 1981 and rest on the charism of the testimony of the six young visionaries. They have submitted their witness to the world at large and still continue to submit their experiences. At first, their witness was met with scepticism, ill will and even hostility by the Church and the State. During the past years, the phenomenon of the visionaries has been examined from many angles. Today we can say confidently that the witness of the visionaries is unfailingly humble and joyful, confident and unobtrusive, devoid of theatrics or gushing emotions, without over-emphasis or exaggeration.

WE HAVE SEEN THE MADONNA

What the visionaries are really saying is very simple: we have seen the Madonna. They see not just anything, but the Mother of God - the ''Gospa'' in Croation. The apparitions have ceased for two of the original six visionaries, at Christmas 1982, for Mirjana Dragicevic, and on May 7, 1985, for Ivanka Ivankovic. The other visionaries are Vicka Ivankovic, Marija Pavlovic, Ivan Dragicevic and Jakov Colo. Their words and faces show that they are not lying and are not victims of deception. News of the apparitions to the youths spread like wildfire, and only a few days after the first apparitions thousands of curious sensation seekers or miracle-seeking people came to Medugorje. The number of visitors grew from day to day and the authorities were at a loss to know how to deal with them. They not only feared but even suspected that a Croation counterrevolution was under way.

The children were interrogated by the police. They underwent physical and psychiatric examinations by physicians and were found to be in good health. The only explanation the police could offer can be summed up in one word: mass hysteria! Subsequently, the police declared the mount where the apparitions were occurring, Mount Crnica, as off limits, because of the crowds. The apparitions then took place in private homes and in the fields, then later in the parish church and currently in the rectory of Medugorje.

EUCHARIST BECAME THE FOCAL POINT OF DAILY EVENTS

The pastor at the time, Fr. Jozo Zavko, was baffled by the phenomenon, being fearful of the possibility of extraneous manipulation or suggestion. But, after many clarifying conversations with the visionaries and the local Ordinary, and after long prayer, Fr. Jozo concluded that the hand of God was evident and the events were genuine. At his direction, the stream of pilgrims and visitors was channeled into the church where the Eucharist, accompanied by long prayers and powerful evangelistic preaching stressing conversion and prayer, became the focal point of the daily events.

The apparitions occur generally in a set pattern, although the visionaries do not know whether the Gospa will appear or not. An Austrian pilgrim, a spiritual director in a junior seminary, testing the experience for himself, describes his impressions at the moment of the apparition as follows: ''We prayed with the visionaries, each one of us in his own language. Suddenly, the youths fell silent and knelt down. Vicka was kneeling within my narrow field of vision in such

Jakov, Ivanka, Marija

Vicka, Ivan and Marija

The visionaries are open, humble and modest; the ecstasies are devoid of any unnatural features.

Jakov, Ivanka and Marija

Ivan, Jakov, and Marija

*The witness of the visionaries in unfailingly humble &
joyful, confident & unobtrusive, devoid of theatrics or
gushing emotions, without overemphasis or exaggeration.*

a manner that her face, several feet away, was level with my eyes. I can describe only inadequately what her face reflected during the minutes of the apparition. It will remain unforgetable for the rest of my life. She was listening with profound attention. Her face displayed an expression of total self-abandonment and a devotion which absorbed her whole being. Suddenly an expression, resembling a joyous surprise, appeared on her face and her lips formed inaudible words. It was completely silent in the chapel. I could not take my eyes from Vicka. Never before have I seen more beauty in a face, and that on a person who did not stand out among others as being particularly beautiful. I felt as though I were capturing, as if through a mirror, a beauty which does not exist in this world... There have been more important days in my life..., but I received my profoundest experience in Medugorje.'' If, with appropriate justification, apparitions are described as a reflection of the Eternal Light,[2] then the visionaries' faces display something of this Eternal Light according to the testimony of many people who have observed them during the apparitions.

THE MESSAGE OF MEDUGORJE

More important than the observation and the appearance
of the visionaries and their shared experience, and much more
important than the apparitions themselves, are the messages
conveyed to the visionaries by the ''Gospa.'' The apparitions
are extraordinary signs given in difficult times, in crisis-laden
eras which need prophetic words, stirring messages and
admonitions. The main message of Medugorje can be defined
simply. On the third day of the apparitions, it came forth
in one word, repeated tearfully and emphatically three times:
peace, peace, peace. In subsequent apparitions the Mother
of God described herself as the ''Queen of Peace.'' The peace
she refers to is a peace which can be achieved only through
personal and universal repentance, prayer, penance, fasting
and a deeply rooted faith. These are the elements which lead
to true peace in oneself as well as in the world. For peace,
which is written today almost everywhere in capital letters,

Conversion and penance are best expressed through the confession of sins. A stream of grace urges people into the confessional.

...the Eucharist became the focal point of daily events.

can in no way be attained through worldwide peace move-
ments or demonstrations. The word ''peace'' expresses the
complete message of Jesus. ''Peace'' is at one and the same
time the external expression of God's will and the desire of
the war-ravaged peoples of the earth.

REPENTANCE, PRAYER, PENANCE, FASTING

The human countenance in today's world is shadowed in many respects. The world experiences an obscuring of God's face. Panic and tremendous anxiety have taken hold of people and are spreading everywhere. Man longs for an earthly, utopian paradise. People are uprooted, homeless. And it is in such disoriented times, times devoid of grace, that we experience Mary's visitation as a heavenly sign which tells us that peace, love, grace, and mercy do really exist. Mary, the woman received into Heaven body and soul, glorified and enjoying the fullness of life, has come to tell us of this Divine life of grace, a life which can be obtained only through our being receptive to it and through our listening to God's Word and will.

The message of conversion, penance, reparation, prayer and the recitation of the rosary are both common and specific

Jozo Zovko

Tomislav Vlasic

Tomislav Pervan

Slavko Barbaric

Petar Ljubicic

Ivan Dugandzic

Franciscan friars associated with St. James Parish.

The number of visitors grew from day to day.

in all the apparitions of Mary to date, especially Fatima and Lourdes. In Medugorje, however, fasting has received special attention.

MARY IS THE PROPHET OF CONVERSION

The central point of Mary's messages is conversion. It is not just coincidence that Mary appeared here on June 24th, 1981, feast of St. John the Baptist, the herald of the Lord and the greatest preacher of conversion. It is in a conversion context that Mary has come. She is the prophet of conversion for the waning second millenium after Christ, to whom she points with all her being. For Mary, conversion means turning to her Son, to God. We must turn to Him and away from godlessness, self destruction and materialism. Mary's way to conversion is that of the Sermon on the Mount: prayer, fasting, living faith, trust in God and all the other great themes of Jesus' exhortation which guide us in following him.

Today, for many, prayer has been widely forgotten and neglected or it has become lukewarm. We are living with a prayer deficit. The constant admonition and call to prayer emphasize a significant characteristic of the life of Jesus. All those who want to stand in the presence of the Son of God must keep watch and pray at all times (Lk 21.36). Furthermore, prayer has a transfiguring effect (see Lk 9.29). Prayer, as an expression of faith, is merely the other side of conversion. Whoever repents and turns toward God must lend expression to his repentance and faith. Through sincere prayer we place God, Jesus, at the center of our lives. The Madonna tells us that the minimum amount of daily prayer should be the Credo and seven times the Our Father, Hail Mary and Glory Be. The apparitions in Medugorje add the advice to pray the entire rosary in order to penetrate the fundamental mysteries of the life of Jesus and one's own faith. *The rosary represents a living connection with the gospel of the Lord.*

Conversion and penance are best expressed through the confession of sins. Medugorje is renowned for the many general confessions which are made here. A stream of grace, an invisible force, urges people into the confessional. This grace does not remain without its effects.

FASTING PROMOTES OUR
READINESS TO PRAY

Fasting, too, is emphasized at Medugorje. Today, fasting, as a way of disciplining the body and mind, is recommended by scientists. Some people actually suggest that global fasting

Vicka greeting pilgrims.

should be proclaimed in order to save the earth, that part of Creation entrusted to mankind, from man, the fifth horseman of the Apocalypse. Fasting promotes our readiness to pray, enhances our receptivity to grace, and enables us to take faith seriously. It has sanctifying and healing effects on man's spiritual and bodily structure. The whole gospel is included in these messages and in them we can read the heavenly pastoral plan for the world. Mary's way is the path to the Lord. Mary promotes the gifts of the Holy Spirit, awakens dormant or atrophied charisms, rekindles baptismal grace and stirs the life of grace into a shining fire, which then consumes and spreads to others.

MARY'S MESSAGE IS A PURE ECHO OF THE GOSPEL

Mary's pastoral work is first and foremost concerned with peace. She is the answer to the yearning of mankind today and the great sign from Heaven (Rev 12:1) which points to the imminent, final coming of the Lord in all His splendor. ''The message of Medugorje has been seen as a serious warning from Heaven to our world which is in the process of destroying itself. The openness and profound seriousness with which she has been received by local residents and

Visionaries relating Mary's call to prayer, conversion, fasting and penance to a group of pilgrims.

millions of pilgrims is profoundly stirring. The message is a call to prayer, conversion and fasting and its purpose is to give this violent world, which is governed by might, a new direction. Viewed from this perspective the message is a pure echo of the gospel."[3]

The role of the Mother of God in Medugorje is a prophetic one also. Prophets do not discern primarily the future and they do not predict, but rather they explain and interpret the message of God. They are heralds of the will of God and they call for repentance in troubled times. They offer no new revelation, but lend validity to and confirm emphatically already existing revelation. Faith must be deepened, relationships with God must be purified and love of one's neighbor must be integrated and lived.

Mary's entire life constantly reveals prophetic features: her suffering, her disregard of pain, all the moments of her life. Her service has not yet ended; as virgin-mother she remains the servant of the work of salvation of her Son and continues to function as a mediatrix in the Church. Thus, the apparitions are relevant for our times, for threatening words are heard in our world, dark clouds are rising on the horizon, dangers are planetary in scope, human dignity and values are trampled under foot, consciousness of sin and the need for redemption have faded. The apparitions represent God's care and concern for the human soul, a call from the heavens to earth, the Divine response to the cries of our times.

THE IMPACT OF THE APPARITIONS AND THE MESSAGES

The message proclaimed through the apparitions of the Mother of God has had a tremendous impact on the lives of the visionaries, the parish and people generally. People were reached in the totality (of life); first they were frightened, then came renewal, change and the reversal of life styles. This is the best proof that the soil was receptive, and that the message did not resound in a lifeless vacuum.

It did not take long for human reaction to respond to Divine action. From the very beginning the reaction was overwhelming and continues unabated. Though during the first days curiosity and sensationalism may have played a role, everything was transformed into tremendous, powerful, fruitful evangelization, a readiness to repent, and the receiving of the Sacraments by the masses of pilgrims. These subsequent events involving the people interpret, define and cast

The celebration of the feast of the Exaltation of the Cross (Sept. 14) brings thousands of pilgrims.

a clear light on the initial event. No human agency has expected or imagined the initial spark. The first impetus must be seen and interpreted in the light of the strong, continuous wave of repentance, the deepening of faith and prayer. The Archbishop of Split, Msgr. Dr. Frane Franic, stated in an interview in 1983 that the events in Medugorje have done more to promote faith in two years than traditional ministry had accomplished during the forty post-war years. The results have been positive in every respect and, therefore, it is reasonable to take a positive and openminded stance toward the events.

FAITH IS IN OPERATION IN MEDUGORJE

In Medugorje people are not filled with propaganda, in which case the authenticity of Mary's apparitions would be stressed and attempts made to prove such authenticity; instead, the people are confronted with the claims of the gospel. Today mankind is saturated with posters of heroes who promise much but have nothing to give. In Medugorje it is possible to point to fruitful results which lead us to the conviction that the initial event was authentic. Throughout Church history, the faithful's conviction has been, and remains to this day, an agency collaborating in the formulation of the faith which is to be embraced. Here we witness the right of the ordinary man to have his say concerning the fate of the world, his duty to counter evil and to fight it. No new truth is being proclaimed in Medugorje; rather, the truth of the gospel is being spelled out. Faith is in operation here, in everyday life, not in empty rhetoric or lipservice. Since the entire Church is enjoined to evangelize, this task is accepted conscientiously in Medugorje. The Church concretises her mission and identity through this conscious evangelization of the world. The Christian faith resists any form of elitism for it is the faith of the ordinary people, accessible to everyone and livable. The message enunciated in Medugorje has been heard, understood and received, not as non-binding teaching or mere phraseology, but as praxis which affects and endues our way of life with prayer, fasting, and readiness for reconciliation, in frequent monthly confession, almost daily church attendance and reception of the Eucharist, with matchless hospitality and love.

No man is forever protected from or immunized against the onslaught of evil. Here and there in Medugorje, there are manifestations of fatigue. This also happened to the author of the Book of Revelation, when he sent his letters to the communities of Asia Minor. Heaven cannot be reached in a forced march. It is always necessary to warn against exaggerations, and it takes a large measure of pastoral wisdom to accommodate the charism of discernment from the Holy Spirit. Therefore, pastoral work avoids everything spectacular, effusive, enthusiastic or extraordinary in such matters. A premium is placed on sober, devout and internally rooted service of God;[4] from this basis it spreads to other parishes at home and abroad. In Medugorje the dominant features of religious life are naturalness and clarity, equanimity and freedom, devotion to love and long daily prayers. More than a thousand people gather here every day; on weekends several thousand come and on High Holy Days more than ten thousand congregate in Medugorje.

The implantation of apparitions in a nation of varied faiths and denominations is also bearing ecumenical fruit. In Medugorje Catholics, Orthodox and Moslems come together to honor the same "Gospa." The renowned mariologist, Abbe Laurentin was able to state in his final judgement in his book about Medugorje[5] that Mary's apparitions in Medugorje were fulfilling their innate function and that his own ideas concerning the apparitions had been corroborated in Medugorje.

An expression, resembling a joyous surprise, appeared on her (Vicka) face and her lip's formed inaudible words.

CRITERIA OF ECCLESIATSICAL VERIFICATION

The aforementioned judgement by Laurentin raises at once the question concerning the criteria employed in assessing the authenticity of apparitions and private revelations. First of all, there must be complete congruence with the Church's magisterium. In no way can an apparition or private revelation rescind already existing revelation or maintain its opposite. Apparitions serve only to clarify and illustrate. Since the subject of apparitions is susceptible to errors, imagination and fanaticism,[6] it is necessary to investigate (test) the visionaries' psychological, physical and religious conditions. Personal holiness of the visionary is not a prerequisite; however, serious "moral deficiencies of the person are an unfavorable factor affecting the issue of recognizing the authenticity of a revelation, though they are not taken as a negative criterion as a matter of principle as are, however, mendacity and lack of modesty. On the other hand, a certain moral heroism, especially humility, self-control, love of the Cross, service to fellow man, reserve, and dignity are evaluated positively."[7] Incidental or accompanying errors are not necessarily considered as negative criteria.[8] If, however, the subject rejects all manner of ecclesiastical investigation, or if the person in question insists stubbornly on his opinion, "then this will be interpreted as a definite sign of self-delusion."[9] The following are negative criteria relied upon in denying the authenticity of private revelations: statements about the emission of sins, predictions of visions of God (by particular individuals at specific times), proclamations "concerning the state of grace of a particular living or deceased person or his damnation, whenever ... matters of a secular nature are communicated, e.g. concerning an illness, court trials, certain scientific controversies or a political issue. This position rests on the conviction that apparitions, by their very nature, address themselves to the Kingdom of God and are not meant to serve curiosity and the secular security of the individual."[10]

In the case of Medugorje the behavior of ecclesiastical authorities has been according to the Church's practice in analogous cases. The bishop has allowed himself to be guided by the gift of discernment and reasonable caution, assuming, by and large, a wait-and-see attitude. In his first clarifying public statement, published on August 6th, 1981 in "Glas

Koncila'' (Voice of the Council), the Ordinary took a bold position, defending the visionaries, the Franciscan friars, the faithful and the faith itself against attacks and defamations by the official media. He did not exclude the possibility of the apparitions actually happening. In January 1982 he established a commission for the investigation of the phenomenon. The commission was enlarged by an additional member in the spring of 1983. The guiding principle in these actions was to avoid precipitous action, lest (the case of) any party be harmed.[11] In the meantime, the bishop has voiced some reservations which, however, should not be interpreted as a definitive judgement on Medugorje. Whenever the eternal Light appears, casting its reflection on the dark mirror of the world, all arguments, pro and con, have to be weighed carefully instead of focusing merely on the negative.

On May 2, 1986, the investigation by the commission was brought to an end. The individual members submitted their ''vote'' and personal reports to the Bishop who, in turn, took everything to Joseph Cardinal Ratzinger and the Congregation of the Faith in Rome. In the meantime, Cardinal Ratzinger has offered the Bishop the support and assistance of the Congregation in any future investigations. Ultimately, it will rest with the local Bishop to make a definitive statement concerning the apparitions. By the fruits, Medugorje will be authenticated.

In the light of Church teaching and practice, Medugorje

Vicka, Ivan, Marija praying with the Madonna during an apparition.

presents no problems. Many priests, bishops and lay people continue to journey to Medugorje to experience for themselves the blessings and the peace promised by the Gospa. The focus in Medugorje is not so much Mary per se; rather, everything is Christ-centered since each gathering flows into a Eucharistic gathering. The visionaries are open, humble and modest; the ecstasies are devoid of any unnatural features. The visions begin with amazing synchronism. During the apparitions the visionaries have been subjected to various medical examinations. Electrodes attached to their eyelids recorded simultaneity during the sudden focusing of their eyes on the same point. The greatest difference was two tenths of a second. The transmission of sound through headsets and exposure to blinding light elicited no reactions during the apparitions though, under normal conditions, the visionaries do react normally. Moreover, subjection to pin pricks and elevations of their bodies during the moments of ecstasy provoked no reaction. "No symptoms of catatonia could be observed - neither a tensing of the muscles, nor contortions or rigidity. There is no jerking of the head ... there is no evidence of heightened emotional activity heading for a climax."[12] The encephalogram has proven that the ecstasies do not represent dreamlike or epileptic states. Medical experiments, however, are only useful to a process of elimination indicating which phenomena or conditions can be excluded. Thus, e.g. hypotheses suggesting hallucination, dreaming, epilepsy and suggestion cannot be proven. The real object of the visions, the Gospa, is not amenable to scientific experimentation. We concur with the assessment of Father Michael Scanlan, T.O.R., of the Franciscan University of Steubenville (Ohio, USA), which he conveyed to the pastor of Medugorje and to the bishop of Mostar: "I observed the visionaries twice while the apparitions were occuring. The only explanation of their behavior that can be offered is that they are captivated by a supernatural phenomenon of a mystical nature. There is no hint of (psychic) hallucinations. The only tenable explanation is that we are indeed dealing with an apparition of Mary, the Mother of God, as attested by the children."[13]

APPEARANCES OF THE HOLY VIRGIN AND THEIR MEANING

When considering apparitions of Our Lady, we enter into dim theological territory; an area where we may encounter rejection or ill feeling among some theologians and among the main branches of theology. Why is this so? Is the rejection due to the ambivalence of such a pheonomenon as an ''apparition?'' During the past fifty years, more than two hundred and thirty such phenomena have been recorded; yet none has received ecclesiastical approval.

The Church seems to be traumatized by apparitions, living with the fear that everything may be grounded in deception. Is it perhaps that those with the task of considering the evidence have not been receptive enough to the reality? This situation is confusing and the causes need to be identified. Perhaps it has something to do with the historical-critical method or with an excessively rationalistically oriented philosophy and theology. Predominant in contemporary church structures and in theology we have a purely intellectual and legalistic mentality which "is biased with regards to abstraction and practicality,"[14] and which considers apparitions as being meaningless and superfluous. Systematic theology declares apparitions to be unnecessary and insignificant, based on suppositions. In fundamental theology apparitions are excluded as a useful object of study. Scientific exegesis "holds up biblical revelation as the inspired Word, whose author is God, against all later revelations."[15]

Although today we do have a rather developed Marian theology, and Council statements testify that Mary contains within herself all the mysteries of faith, yet theology and mariology have failed to grant a firm place, a settled home, to apparitions. Instead, apparitions of Mary are being discounted consistently. The reason for this may be the exaltation of human reason. Sense experiences and feelings have become relativised and therefore, are scorned as partaking in the realm of shadows, the irrational, and unbridled fantasy.[16] Modern psychology, psychoanalysis and deterministic thinking, which prohibit God from revealing Himself in the world, may also have influenced the rejection.

In any event, the treatment of this issue has been unfortunate. It is not beyond possibility that the Church, on her way through today's world, may have been diverted from something essential, a road sign, out of fear of the growing incidence of prophecies or because of her inflexible structures.

The subject of "apparitions" lingers also on the peripheries of mystical and spiritual theology, perhaps because apparitions are concerned with the sensible, the sensuous, and the visionary. The question, therefore, arises as to the existence, in present day seminaries and theological faculties, of teachers and masters of the spiritual life capable of communicating to others the truth about authentic religious experiences. Where are religious experiential phenomena to be dealt with? Perhaps they are touched upon peripherally here and there in connection with discussions of deviant practices, the occult, magic and spiritism, while genuine Christian experiences, the charismatic experiences considered normal in the early Church, are being excluded. Apparitions do belong to the realm of the charismatic, since the visionaries do not elect themselves to be visionaries, but are merely recipients of a heavenly manifestation or message.

The basis of all apparitions is the Easter Apparition of the resurrected Lord. Apparition experiences are always very personal and subjective. They are experiences which, for all practical purposes, lie beyond our scrutiny and verification by objective and empirical means. "They are intended to link the invisible world with man's sensitive nature, in adaptation to the latter. Christian revelation, grounded in the Incarnation respects and does not scorn the body and the senses."[17]

People come, see and experience and return home as missionaries of the Gospel message given through Mary, the Queen of Peace.

A village family at prayer. The Madonna has asked for family prayer, the rosary, daily mass, penance and fasting.

Consequently, apparitions of the Mother of God belong to the realm of subjective religious experience and, writing about them, we must resort to analogies. Just as God did not let Jesus appear to all the people, "but only to the witnesses pre-selected by God: to us, who ate and drank with Him after His resurrection from the dead" (Rev 10.41f), so the Mother of God appears only to individual persons, those the Lord has chosen as witnesses.

The same God who spoke in biblical revelation speaks also in and through apparitions. Apparitions do not deal with new revelation but are intended to revitalise the original revelation, and to recall what once, in the history of the world, had been illuminated in Jesus Christ. Apparitions rather actualize, explain, elucidate, awaken, stimulate, and give new impulse to the process of faith-building. No new truths are proclaimed and no additions to the existing treasure of faith are promulgated. Apparitions are addressed to the life and conduct of man. They deal more with hope than with faith; they aim at the goal and the future.[18]

The messages proclaimed in apparitions are always only a close echo, a reflection of the message of Jesus Christ, given in light of the conditions of the contemporary world. The messages are designed to stimulate us to change, "to break the circle of entrenched habits, and to strengthen afresh our faith, prayer and dialogue with God."[19]

Why does Mary appear today? If we look at Mary's role in the history of salvation, we can see her prophetic charism. The Munich dogmatist, L. Scheffczyk, emphasises: ''that apparitions of Mary, representing evidence of motherly affection toward those who stand in a special salvation situation in place of the entire human race, convey illumination and knowledge to the on-going history of mankind, which ultimately emanate from the light of Christ and the glory of God.''[20]

The recent upsurge of charismatic experiences within the Church is a sign of the work of the Holy Spirit in which the gospel is emphatically discovered anew. This is also the purpose of the apparitions of Mary. Viewed from this perspective, Christians who have had charismatic experiences or Christians consciously committed to renewal are, perhaps, the strongest endorsers of the authenticity of Marian apparitions. In every age, the Spirit takes possession of, empowers and sends forth certain human beings to recall forgotten truths and to write a new chapter in the history of the Church. Mary, who was assumed into heaven body and soul is, perhaps, most called upon in the Divine schema to promulgate the necessity of living the gospel, lest faith be degraded into something anemic and without heart.

Perhaps the Church's scepticism toward the generally not recognized apparitions is related to a latent fear of a new prophetic wave, or of the decadence associated with things enthusiastic and charismatic which have traumatized the history of the Church.

We must take care not to emphasize abstract thinking only, or to value only intellectual achievement, while excluding symbolism, signs, dreams, visions and utopian aspirations, or labeling them by-products of fantasy. Nor should we explain apparitions as being hallucinations or impulsiveness on part of the visionaries. For, in doing so we would excise a few valuable chapters from the gospel.

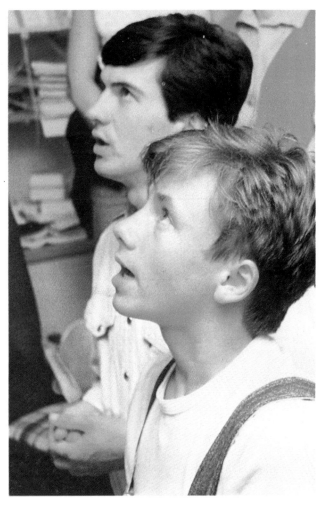

Ivan and Jakov

Visions begin with amazing synchronism.

CONCLUSION

Thus far Medugorje has presented the universal Church with many valuable and positive gifts. Something, whatever it may be, is happening in Medugorje, that exercises a centripetal, attracting, magnetic influence on the pilgrims. It works unobtrusively. In Medugorje one senses piety, commitment to God, the sanctity of the apparition room, simplicity of the surroundings, a divine power - a palpable grace - which announces itself and captivates. In Medugorje, many experience a new, a sacred awe before the "mysterium tremendum et fascinosum" (tremendous and fascinating mystery).

One thing, however, should not be tolerated in Medugorje: resentment toward the matter itself, the visionaries or even the pilgrims. No ideologized judgements should be rendered. The visionaries are to be protected from defamation, as long as serious culpability or mendacity cannot be proven. They

are entitled to protection, priestly support, spiritual guidance
designed to lead them to orderliness, fulfillment of their
obligations, prayer and, above all, humility. We should pray
and hope that prudence, sound human reason and the Holy
Spirit shall prevail. In all matters we should be guided by
the apostle's advice: "Do not extinguish the Spirit. Do not
disdain prophetic words. Examine everything and hold on
to whatever is good" (Thes 5.19-21). Satan and his intrigues
must be unmasked (see Rev 13.6; 16.1 ff). It is necessary
to make a discernment among the spirits. Such power of
discernment should be requested from God for all those who
bear responsibility for Medugorje. Everything spiritual and
of the Holy Spirit can only be recognized and adjudged
spiritually and through the power of the divine Spirit. Any
partiality must be precluded. Let us allow the search for and
discovery of truth to emanate from the ranks, the (ordinary)
people. As is said in *Lumen Gentium:* "The exercise of the
episcopal magisterium takes place in a multifaceted exchange
of faith with the faithful, priests and theologians" (No. 51).
Simple members of the Church are the witnesses and bearers
of rekindled faith and of that kind of peace which can only
be obtained through prayer, fasting, repentance and penance.
These are the only instruments which can offer us a hopeful
future and save us from self-destruction. This is the main
task of a true mother and also the task of the heavenly mother,
Mary. It is in this realm that the fact of apparitions of the

Mother of God has to be placed. It represents a feature of our burdened times, the continuing sound of the symphony of heavenly tunes in their infinite and unfathomable variations on the only theme: God's care for His creation, and above all for mankind.

The pilgrim is offered the evangelic way, the way of prayer and fasting, peace and love.

Appendix

PILGRIMAGE

To speak about Medugorje is to speak about the millions and endless streams of believers (and non-believers) who are flowing daily into this holy place. We ask, what is the power which forces a person to a long and sometimes unknown journey into a foreign country? What kind of energy urges a person to go on a pilgrimage (to Medugorje)?

Man's subconscience, where an undistructable longing for God is rooted, manifests itself in the form of indistinct aspirations, desires and dreams. Spiritual and mental incentives break through, like a chicken in an egg, to see the light of day, compelled by the whisperings of the heart rather than by knowledge of the mind. And so the soul of man searches.

As we observe the pilgrims in Medugorje, we see this same spiritual process at work. In spite of a warm home with all its comforts, and a quiet chapel or church in which to pray and glorify God to their heart's content, the pilgrims come, driven by these inexplicable forces, bearing the burdens of travel and often the hardships of walking. Pilgrims come for various reasons: psychological needs, illness, burdens, vows; to pray for this or that, and even for the sake of a "pilgrimage" itself, many times not knowing exactly why they have come. The pilgrim has a need to glorify God by walking, traveling, moving forward to an instinctive goal.

Like the Jewish people, displaced and scattered all over the world, who instinctively long for their "Jerusalem", the city of God, the sanctuary and homeland of their spirit, so the pilgrim to Medugorje. "Jerusalem", the totality of all that the Jews desire, expect, or humanly long for, is a universal notion of the finality of human existence. "Jerusalem" is the place of longing and, as the destination of a journey, is proof that pilgrimaging belongs to the essence of a person's soul, to the deepest longings of the human heart.

We can liken the pilgrim to the men and women of faith spoken of in the Letter to the Hebrews, "By acknowledging themselves strangers and foreigners..., they showed that they were seeking a homeland ... they were longing for a better home, a heavenly one" (Heb 11:13-14).

In making a pilgrimage, a person realizes elementary tanscience and exposure, vulnerability and the uncertainty of this life. "Pilgrimage" is like an island, a space where, cut off from the natural conveniences of everyday life, we meet God. Many life confessions, deeply moving conversions to the loving God, take place in pilgrim places. In Medugorje, too.

Pilgrims are God seekers, and in seeking God, they find their true self. We cannot separate the experience of God and the experience of self, for each person bears within himself what makes him or her a personality, an individual unique in the history of creation, the image of the invisible God. In meeting God, the pilgrim meets his own run-away heart. In Medugorje, too.

In the wide spectrum of God's special interventions into the course of man's endeavours, Medugorje is only another obvious proof that the pilgrim is in essence a religious being. He or she simply cannot do without God. The pilgrim wishes, one way or another, to soar up to God, to reach God. Unconscious faith becomes conscious, the unexpressed becomes verbalized, unsteady conviction grows into a firm decision to live up to the obligations of the baptismal vow, and individual prayer flows into universal prayer for the Church and her needs.

From the first days, everything in Medugorje has been directed towards the evangelization of the faithful, towards bringing Jesus Christ and his message into the pilgrim's heart. In Medugorje, nobody is offered a cheap recipe for all the hardships or crosses, a cheap solution for all problems, or a cheap medicine for every illness. What is offered may seem most insignificant in life to some: conversion, restructuring of values, reconsideration of attitudes, redirecting of life tracks, in order to achieve peace, to recover, and to be healed. The unpleasant is offered: self denial, the cross, the way of Jesus. Nobody is offered a magic formula or a pill for happiness, but rather *the pilgrim is offered the evangelic way, the way of prayer and fasting, peace and love.* The way that is offered is the way Jesus Christ, the lover of man's happiness, of the purity of man's heart and environment, spoken of long before today's fighters against environmental pollution. Long before today's demagogues or prophets, political or partyleaders, God raised, and through his word is still raising His voice that it is necessary to change the course of the life's ship is we want to live fully and not just survive. He says there is no easy road to happiness. Happiness is in conversion and it is in conversion that the whole message of Medugorje is built. Medugorje wants to shake us out of indifference toward the message of Jesus.

In the history of our world and Christianity, when the Christian faith became the official religion, little by little, faith lost its power and its authenticity. Persons who wanted to be authentic Christians went into the Egyptian deserts and became monks. Their goal was not to become monks, but rather to be authentic Christians. Persons who wanted to experience authentic Christianity followed them to the desert. They were pilgrims from other countries who traveled to the

Egyptian desert to experience a living faith. They went back to their countries and became missionaries. So in Medugorje. People come, see and experience and return home as missionaries of the Gospel message given through Mary, the Mother of God, the Queen of Peace.

ENDNOTES

1. Much has been written about the phenomenon of Medugorje throughout the world and in different ways. The body of publications is growing daily, including audio and video recordings. Printed material about Medugorje is too copious to be reviewed here. There exist many publications in Italian, French, German, English and Portuguese, as well as Polish, Czech, Slovenian, Japanese and Arabic. Some work is in preparation even in Iceland, Indeed, the phenomenon has reached the most important languages of contemporary civilization and the avalanche of publications is unstoppable.

2. Title of a book published by German Rovira: Der Widerschein des Ewigen Liches. Marienerscheinungen und Gnadenbilder als Zeichen der Gotteskraft (Reflection of the Eternal Light. Marian Apparitions and Symbols of Grace as Signs of Divine Power), Kevelaer 1984.

3. René Laurentin/Ljudevit Rupčić, Das Geschehen von Medugorje. Eine Untersuchung (The Events of Medugorje. An Examination), Graz-Wien-Këln 1985, 15.

4. Laurentin/Rupčić, ibid. 144-170 passim

5. Laurentin/Rupčić, ibid. 162.

6. René Laurentin, Marienerscheinungen (Marian Apparitions), in: W. Beinert/ H. Petri, Handbuch der Marienkunde (Handbook of Mariology), Regensburg 1984, pp. 528-555, 552.

7. Josef Schumacher, Privatoffenbarungen und Marienverehrung. Fundamental theologische Überlegungen, in: ROVIRA (see ref. 2), 66-88,74).

8. Schumacher, ibid. 74.

9. Schumacher, ibid. 74.

10. Schumacher, ibid. 74.

11. Also among the ranks of highly-placed Church authorities it has both its enthusiastic and influential supporters and its powerful enemies. For a good many it is a sign from heaven; for others, however, it is seen as a mad creation or cunning machination hatched by wily Franciscans in Medugorje, from which the „charismatic movement" has grown in strength. Opponents of Medugorje have lumped it with something quite separate – the conflict that has been going on for years in the diocese of Herce-govina between secular and religious clergy. Thus right from the start the whole Medugorje phenomenon con-cerning the apparitions has been considered unauthentic and non-factual.

12. Laurentin/Rupčić, ibid. 147. Should anybody wish to enter more deeply into the medical and scientific experi-ments conducted on the visionaries of Medugorje or to gather more information about them, they ought to read the book written jointly by Professor H. Joyeux and René Laurentin, Etudes médicales et scientifiques sur les apparitions de Medugorje, Paris, O. E. I. L. 1985.

13. Laurentin/Rupčić, ibid. 156.

14. Rene Laurentin, „Marian Apparitions" (see ref. 6), 542.

15. Laurentin, ibid. 542f.

16. Laurentin, ibid. 543.

17. Laurentin, ibid. 539.

18. Laurentin, ibid. 541.

19. Laurentin, ibid. 542.

20. Leo Scheffczyk, Die theologischen Grundlagen von Er-scheinungen und Prophezeiungen (Theological Founda-tions of Apparitions and Prophecies), Leutesdorf 1982, p. 25.